Sam, Say God is the Love Blessings Mile 2018

You Can Choose to Say No

Every day when you wake up, you will hear two voices. One voice is Jesus, the One who came to give you life more abundantly, and one is Satan's, the one who came to kill, steal, and destroy (John 10:10).

This book is designed, through daily prayer and reading of the accompanying Scripture references, to give you the power and the ability to choose which voice you will say yes to.

Merle M. Mills

You Can Choose to Say No

Content design by Evelyn J. Wagoner

ISBN #:13:978-0-9886 162-3-3

To my God,
thank You for loving me
and forgiving me.
As long as You give me breath,
I will serve You.

To my family,
thank you for supporting me
by giving me the freedom
of many hours at my computer.

To those who generously support,
share your God-given talents, and pray for me,
thank you.

Contents

Introduction 1
Lack of Faith 2
Lying... 3
Envy... 4
Dishonesty 5
Debt 6
Pornography 7
Not Reading the Bible 8
Alcohol 9
Unforgiveness 10
Disrespect 11
Anger.. 12
Fear 13
Gossip... 14
Not Praying ....ₐ................... 15
Disorganization 16
Disobedience to Parents... 17
Abortion 18
Wasting Time 19
Not Dressing for Success.. 20
Not Studying 21
Hopelessness 22
Peer Pressure 23
Not Sharing Your Faith.. 24
Loneliness 25
Age Limitation... 26
Lack of Confidence.. 27
Anxiety 28
Impurity 29
Bad Manners... 30
Not Feeling Loved 32
The Greatest Relationship 33
About the Author... 34

Introduction

For years, I had no idea of my true identity until I began to read what my Heavenly Father said about me in the Holy Scriptures. Those truths freed me from the opinion of others and changed my life in such a powerful way that I wanted to share them with those who would dare to read—and dare to believe—them.

If you have picked up this book, it is your time for transformation. My prayer is that as you read each page and memorize what our Heavenly Father says about you, you will discover who you are: valuable … precious … special … God's prized creation. You can have the God-given power to say NO to the enemy of your soul.

You Can Choose to Say No to
Lack of Faith

my faith is in You
i know You are there
like the faith i have in the sofa
in the chair i sit on
like the table i place my lunch on
i don't question
the light switch
in my room
like the laws of electricity
i don't question
before i go to bed at night
i don't question whether
my breath will leave or stay
so
why should i not believe
or put my faith in
or say yes
to You?

Don't let your hearts be troubled. Trust in God,
and trust also in Me. (John 14:1)

You brought me safely from my mother's womb and led me
to trust You when I was a nursing infant. (Psalm 22:9)

I will never fail you. I will never abandon you.
(Hebrews 13:5)

And be sure of this: I am with you always,
even to the end of the age. (Matthew 28:20)

You Can Choose to Say No to
Lying

it happens so quickly
in the midst of a situation
or a conversation
it seems necessary
to lie

then i have to lie again
to cover the first lie
then another to cover
the second
now I am in a web
embarrassed that i may
soon be found out

then the trust between me
and others is lost
again

Heavenly Father, save me
so i can say yes to
the web of truth

I am the way, the truth, and the life. No one can come to the
Father except through Me. (John 14:6)

Yes, I am the vine; you are the branches. Those who remain in
Me, and I in them, will produce much fruit. For apart from Me
you can do nothing. (John 15:5)

I have determined that my mouth will not sin.
(Psalm 17:3- GW)

Keep your tongue from evil and your lips
from telling lies. (Psalm 34:13-NIV)

You Can Choose to Say No to
Envy

it means to want
someone else' s possession
something that's not mine
why would I spend the time
wanting what's not mine
it's useless for my frame of mind
so, I decide
to enjoy only what I find
to be mine

A heart at peace gives life to the body, but envy rots the bones. (Proverbs 14:30 NIV)

Love is patient, love is kind. It does not envy, it does not boast, it is not proud. (1 Corinthians 13:4 NIV)

Therefore, rid yourselves of all malice and all deceit, hypocrisy, envy, and slander of every kind.
(1 Peter 2:1 NIV)

You Can Choose to Say No to
Dishonesty

to defraud or deceive
seems like everyone's
doing it
government leaders
athletes
celebrities

let me weigh the factors
small acts lead to big acts
even
lifetime consequences

let me be responsible for
my actions
so i will reap
appropriate
reactions

let me be honest
in all my
interactions

Remove dishonesty from your mouth. Put deceptive speech
far away from your lips. (Proverbs 4:24 GW)

Do not steal. Do not deceive or cheat one another.
(Leviticus 19:11)

Just say a simple, "Yes, I will," or "No, I won't."
Anything beyond this is from the evil one. (Matthew 5:37)

You Can Choose to Say No to
Debt

Any debt, especially credit card debt, is spending today with the intent to pay tomorrow. If the money isn't paid in full within the next 30 days, or minimum payment made, interest and late fees will be added.

During this time, if the card is used, the balance will become higher, increasing the price of the original item or items purchased. Late payments could also affect credit rating, credit history, and future purchasing ability. It is soon out of control. Before spending ask these questions:

Can I afford it?
Have I budgeted for it?
Is it necessary?

Your answers could be the keys to saying yes to living a life free and untangled from debt.

Heavenly Father, restrain me that I may maintain and contain my spending. In Jesus' name, amen.

Just as the rich rule the poor, so the borrower is servant to the lender. (Proverbs 22:7)

The wicked borrow and never repay, but the godly are generous givers. (Psalm 37:21)

Beware! Guard against every kind of greed. Life is not measured by how much you own. (Luke 12:15)

You Can Choose to Say No to
Pornography

it's like poison
your mind is a prize
don't open it to lies

it's like poison
protect your eye gate
before it's too late
watch what you watch
it may take years to erase

it's like poison
leaving behind guilt and shame
don't look
you may become hooked

it's like poison
seek help
tell someone you trust
confess
God will give you
the strength

When you are tempted, He will show you a way out so that
you can endure. (1 Corinthians 10:13)

Give your bodies to God because of all He has done for you.
Let them be a living and holy sacrifice—the kind He will find
acceptable. This is truly the way to worship Him.
(Romans 12:1)

Keep your thoughts on whatever is right or deserves praise:
things that are true, honorable, fair, pure, acceptable, or
commendable. (Philippians 4:8 GW)

I will refuse to look at anything vile and vulgar.
(Psalm 101:3)

You Can Choose to Say No to
Not Reading the Bible

Most decisions, like purchasing an automobile, a computer, or choosing a college, are based on their potential benefit. We also choose to eat certain foods because they contribute to better health. Deciding to read the Bible will produce life-changing results. Here are a few:

you will experience good success (Joshua 1:8)
life and health (Proverbs 4:22)
hope (Psalms 119:114)
understanding (Psalm 119:104)
wisdom (Psalm 119:99)
knowing what God is like (John 5:39)
freedom (John 8:31-32)
a closer relationship with God (James 4:8)
inner strength (Ephesians 3:16)
know God's great love for you (Jeremiah 31:3)
His forgiveness (Micah 7:18-19)
His extravagant sacrifice for you (John 3:16)

Heavenly Father, I thank You for my Bible. As I say yes to read it every day, open my understanding to enjoy the benefits, to see the wondrous plan You have for my life, and to understand the great love You have for me. In Jesus' name, amen.

You Can Choose to Say No to
Alcohol

According to *Psychology Today*, alcohol consumption is associated with many health issues: heart disease, stroke, cancer, liver disease, chemical dependency, pregnancy, sexually transmitted diseases, and alcohol poisoning. There are additional unwanted consequences like death, injuries, assault, date rape, unsafe sex, academic problems, property damages, and police problems ... doing poorly on exams or papers, receiving lower grades or dropping out of school.

Hollywood, commercials, and advertisements make a glass in hand look glamorous. The benefits? None are obvious.

Heavenly Father, help me to preserve this body You gave me. Give me the strength to say no to the pressure of those around me who try to encourage me to drink strong drinks. Help me not fill my body with anything that may alter my thinking ability. In Jesus' name, amen.

Wine produces mockers; alcohol leads to brawls.
Those led astray by drink cannot be wise.
(Proverbs 20:1)

You Can Choose to Say No to
Unforgiveness

you're not forgiving for the other person
you're forgiving for you
they may not be sorry or apologize
that's not your problem
you're forgiving for you
you don't have to let them back
into your life
after all, it's best to avoid strife
and if you do
you're forgiving because
it's the Master's will for your life
He is the example
He forgives you
just because He loves
you.

Be kind to each other, tenderhearted, forgiving one another, just as God through Christ has forgiven you. (Ephesians 4:32)

Do not judge others, and you will not be judged. Do not condemn others, or it will all come back against you. Forgive others, and you will be forgiven. (Luke 6:37)

But if you refuse to forgive others, your Father will not forgive your sins. (Matthew 6:15)

"He who is devoid of the power to forgive is devoid of the power to love." (Martin Luther King Jr.)

You Can Choose to Say No to
Disrespect

nature
traffic lights
the law of gravity
parents
the law of electricity
God
others
are all worthy
of respect
and begin with
respecting one's self.

Show respect to the elderly, and honor older people. In this way you show respect for your God. (Leviticus 19:32 GW)

Everyone must submit to governing authorities, for all authority comes from God, and those in positions of authority have been placed there by God. (Romans 13:1)

Show proper respect to everyone.
(1 Peter 2:17 NIV)

You Can Choose to Say No to
Anger

Heavenly Father, please help me control anger. Don't let me allow situations to ruin my present or future happiness. When I become angry, I'm tempted to make irrational decisions. At times, I become intimidated by what others around me may think. I even become angry when it seems like my back is against the wall. *

My dearest child, whenever you feel anger rising, call to Me. When you are tempted to make irrational decisions, call My name quickly. When it seems your back is against the wall, call My name quietly. I am always with you. I will calm you. I created the anger emotion. I will help you overcome it. My name qualifies you to be instantly filled with peace. I created anger not for you to be led by its influence, but I have given you power to subdue it.—Your Heavenly Father.

Fools vent their anger, but the wise quietly hold it back.
(Proverbs 29:11)

I have given you authority over all the power of the enemy.
(Luke 10:19)

Don't sin by letting anger control you. Think about it overnight and remain silent. (Psalm 4:4)

Don't be quick to get angry, because anger is typical of fools.
(Ecclesiastes 7:9 GW)

Everyone should be quick to listen, slow to speak, and should not get angry easily. (James 1:19 GW)

Don't sin by letting anger control you. (Ephesians 4: 26)

*Prayer by Paris Blount, 14 years old

You Can Choose to Say No to
Fear

fear of the past
fear of the present
fear of the future
fear of situations
fear of failure
fear of people
prevent the joy of
living
now

why allow fear
to rob you?

face it head on
knowing that
God is
with you.

The Lord is my light and my salvation; whom shall I fear?
The Lord is the strength of my life; of whom shall I be afraid?
(Psalm 27:1 KJV)

Don't be afraid, for I am with you. Don't be discouraged, for I
am your God. I will strengthen you and help you. I will hold
you up with My victorious right hand. (Isaiah 41:10)

For God has not given us the spirit of fear; but of power, and
of love, and of a sound mind. (2 Timothy 1:7 KJV)

For He will order His angels to protect you wherever you go.
(Psalm 91:11)

And be sure of this: I am with you always,
even to the end of the age. (Matthew 28:20)

You Can Choose to Say No to

Gossip

One of the definitions of the word gossip is, "a person who habitually reveals personal or sensational facts about others." Sometimes gossiping is also revealing "personal or sensational facts" that have been shared in confidence.

Wildfire destroyed about 500 acres of national forest in California in December 2013. In the book of James, the tongue is described as a fire (James 3:6). If we do not control it, it can spread like a wildfire and destroy lives and the character of others.

Temped to say yes to gossip? Let these words from the Holy Scriptures be your guide to help you say no:

> Take control of what I say, O Lord, and guard my lips.
> (Psalm 141:3)
>
> The words of a gossip are swallowed greedily, and they go down into a person's innermost being. (Proverbs 26:22 GW)
>
> My mouth will speak wise sayings, the insights I have carefully considered. (Psalm 49:3 GW)

Heavenly Father, help me avoid the temptation to gossip. Guard my lips that words of kindness and wisdom may be on my tongue at all times. In Jesus' name, amen.

You Can Choose to Say No to
Not Praying

If you were given the choice of spending an hour with your favorite celebrity or someone you consider very important, who would you choose?

Every day, you have an invitation to spend time with the greatest Person in the universe, the One who created heaven and earth (Genesis 1:1), knows your name (Isaiah 43:1), knows how many hairs are on your head (Matthew 10:30), and knew you before you were formed in your mother's belly (Jeremiah 1:5). Prayer is a conversation with the Greatest Celebrity.

Call to Me and I will answer you and tell you great and unsearchable things you do not know. (Jeremiah 33:3 NIV)

Ask, using My name, and you will receive,
and you will have abundant joy. (John 16:24)

But Jesus often withdrew to the wilderness for prayer.
(Luke 5:16)

I will answer them before they even call to Me.
While they are still talking about their needs,
I will go ahead and answer their prayers! (Isaiah 65:24)

Most invitations request a response. Will you respond with a yes to this one?

Heavenly Father, show me how to give prayer a place of priority in my life. In Jesus' name, amen.

You Can Choose to Say No to
Disorganization

organize shoes
books
clothes
stay free
from clutter
prioritize
clear the mess
put things in their place

keeps your mind free
from stress
makes you
calmer
more productive
destines you
for
success

But be sure that everything is done properly and in order.
(1 Corinthians 14:40)

For everything there is a season, a time for every activity
under heaven. (Ecclesiastes 3:1)

For God is not a God of disorder but of peace.
(1 Corinthians 14:33)

You Can Choose to Say No to
Disobedience to Parents

Do your parents seem overbearing at times? Maybe. It's because they love you and want the best for you. I look back now and realize that much of the advice my parents gave that I thought was irrelevant would have been best for the choices made in my life had I only listened. Some of the decisions I make now are based on the voices of my parents that still ring in my ear today.

> to listen and obey
> mom and dad
> may sometimes seems
> hard
> old fashioned
> don't give a fight
> since
> their advice
> is most likely
> right!

Honor your father and your mother: that your days may be
long upon the land which the Lord your God gives you.
(Exodus 20:12 KJV)

If you honor your father and mother, things will go well for
you, and you will have a long life on the earth.
(Ephesians 6:3 KJV)

My child, listen when your father corrects you.
Don't neglect your mother's instruction. What you learn from
them will crown you with grace and be a chain of honor
around your neck. (Proverbs 1:8-9)

You Can Choose to Say No to
Abortion

at seven weeks
my eyelids seal
to protect my eyes
my ears are complete
I am kicking, and swimming
and am able to
suck my thumb
at eight weeks
I respond to touch
and can feel pain
by the twelfth week
my fingerprints remain
am I a blog of tissue?
the miracle of life
it's the
issue.

The Lord called me before my birth; from within the womb
He called me by name. (Isaiah 49:1)

For the Spirit of God has made me, and the breath of the
Almighty gives me life. (Job 33:4)

Before you were born I set you apart and appointed you as
My spokesman to the world. (Jeremiah 1:5)

You brought me safely from my mother's womb. (Psalm 22:9)

You Can Choose to Say No to
Wasting Time

What does time mean to you?

A 0.94 seconds lead gave Maria Riesch a gold medal during the 2010 Winter Olympics.

A 0.56 lead over Martin Dukurs meant a gold medal for Alexander Tretiakov during Sochi 2014.

0.03 seconds lead over Carmelita Jeter allowed Shelly-Ann Fraser-Pryce to retain her Olympic title in 2012.

Your time is valuable, and how you spend it determines the level of your success. Whether you use it or not, it is still being spent.

As you begin this day, you have 86,400 seconds at your finger tips. Each second is valuable. Will you choose to let each count and spend it wisely?

Until you value yourself, you won't value your time. Until you value your time, you will not do anything with it. (Scott Peck)

Heavenly Father, teach me how to use the time You have given me wisely. In Jesus' name, amen.

Teach us to number each of our days
so that we may grow in wisdom. (Psalm 90:12 GW)

You Can Choose to Say No to

Not Dressing for Success

Today's fashion trend for females suggests low necklines, short skirts, and skimpy shorts. Male trends include sagging waistlines or t-shirts with negative images or slogans. Pink, mint green, blue, purple, green, or rainbow are some of the hair colors chosen by young celebrities.

Your way of dressing sends a message of how you feel about yourself. When you see yourself as your Heavenly Father sees you, you will begin to place value on your appearance, and choose the dress code that will declare that value and self-worth.

Heavenly Father, help me to preserve, protect, honor, and project value in the way I dress. In Jesus' name, amen.

Don't you realize that your body is the temple
of the Holy Spirit, who lives in you and was
given to you by God? You do not belong to yourself,
for God bought you with a high price.
So you must honor God with your body.
(1 Corinthians 6:19-20)

You Can Choose to Say No to
Not Studying

According to an online article, Larry Bird "would shoot more than 300 practice shots before a game." Bird is described as "the best passing and shooting forward in the history of the National Basketball Association."[1]

Another states that Tiger Woods, who has played golf since he was two, continues to spend four-and-a-half hours daily practicing ball striking.[2]

Dominique Dawes rose each morning at five to make the trip to Gaithersburg in time for a two-hour workout before school. After school, she spent an additional five hours in the gym practicing.[3]

Thomas Jefferson, the principal author of the Declaration of Independence wrote, *"I cannot live without books."*

Nelson Mandela, former president of South Africa, once said, *"Education is the most powerful weapon which you can use to change the world ..."*

Study takes commitment, hard work, and determination. You can choose to do it. Your choice will be rewarded with success.

Intelligent people are always ready to learn.
Their ears are open for knowledge.
(Proverbs 18:15)

[1]http://www.perfectshotsshooting.com/basketball-shooting/larry-bird-the-legend-continues/
[2] http://www.best-strategies-for-better-golf.com/tigerwoodspractice.html
[3]http://www.encyclopedia.com/topic/Dominique_Dawes.aspx

You Can Choose to Say No to
Hopelessness

It may begin with depression, despair, expecting something to happen and it doesn't, feeling like no one cares … before you know it, you have slipped into a web of hopelessness. How can you come out it?

Believe in yourself.
Believe you have a future.
Believe that your Heavenly Father has a special plan for your life.
Believe He is reaching out His hands and giving you the gift of hope.

Heavenly Father, please help me out of this hopeless feeling before it becomes a sticky and uncontrollable web. In Jesus' name, amen.

All day long I put my hope in You. (Psalm 25:5)

Our hope is in You alone. (Psalm 33:22)

Your word is my source of hope. (Psalm 119:114)

For I know the plans I have for you, says the Lord.
They are plans for good and not for disaster, to give you a future and a hope. (Jeremiah 29:11)

You Can Choose to Say No to
Peer Pressure

peer pressure can influence
your choice of dress
the food you eat
the music you listen to
even the feelings you feel
I created you to lead
not to follow

I have made you
given you values
instilled them in you

I created you to be the one
to lead not to follow
stand up for
the things you have
been taught
and you know
are right

My Word will guide you
I created you to lead
to change the atmosphere
around you
not to follow
but to be
the example

> Don't copy the behavior and customs of this world,
> but let God transform you into a new person
> by changing the way you think. (Romans 12:2)

> Beloved, follow not that which is evil, but that which is good.
> (3 John 1:11 KJV)

> For I can do everything through Christ, who gives me
> strength. (Philippians 4:13)

You Can Choose to Say No to
Not Sharing Your Faith

When we receive gifts we love and appreciate, we tell others. We have received gifts from God: His goodness, love, and His forgiveness. That good news is worth being shared.

In an interview with *Charisma* magazine, Olympic gold medalist Gabrielle Douglas said, "I love sharing my story and I love sharing about my faith. God has given me this amazing God-given talent, so I'm going to go out and glorify His name."

Tim Tebow boldly painted John 3:16 under his eyes before a college national championship game, and "the next day over 94 million people looked up the verse on internet search engines."[1]

David the Psalmist said: *I will speak to kings about Your laws, and I will not be ashamed.* (Psalm 119:46)

You may not be called to share on such a large level but with the person next to you in class, or the neighbor who always seems sulky, or someone on the school bus who wears thrift-shop clothes. Don't be ashamed. Your faith could give someone's life hope— forever.

Heavenly Father, help me not to feel ashamed of You and all You have done for me. Give me wisdom and boldness to speak about You so others will come to know how much You love and care for them. In Jesus' name, amen.

[1]http://beginningandend.com/standing-tall-jesus-christ-tim-tebows-incredible-season/

You Can Choose to Say No to
Loneliness

my child
whenever you breathe
I am here
there's no need
to feel that
you're alone
or lonely
I am with you
and
I always will be
I am with you
when you question
the past
the present
the future
I am here
and
I always will be
you will never
be alone
for
I will never
never
leave or forsake
you

I will never leave you nor forsake you.
(Joshua 1:5 NIV)

"I am with you always, even to the end of the age."
(Matthew 28:20)

You Can Choose to Say No to
Age Limitation

Louis Braille was 15 years old when he created the Braille writing/reading system.[1]

Phillis Wheatley was 12 years old when she wrote her first poem.[2]

David was a youth when he killed Goliath the giant.[3]

God chose Mary, a young virgin, to be the mother of Jesus the Savior of the world.[4]

You can be used greatly by God as a young person. Your age does not place a limitation on the great plan He has for your life.

Say no to age limitation today and pursue the dream that God has placed in your heart.

With His help, you can achieve great things.

Don't let the excitement of youth cause you to forget your Creator. Honor him in your youth before you grow old and say, "Life is not pleasant anymore." (Ecclesiastes 12:1)

Your young men will see visions. (Joel 2:28)

The span of my years is as nothing before you.
(Psalm 39:5 NIV)

[1,2]http://www.proyouthpages.com/youthhistorymo.html
[3]1 Samuel 17:42
[4]Matthew 1:18

You Can Choose to Say No to
Lack of Confidence

Dear Heavenly Father, there is so much I would like to do, and so many goals I would like to achieve. Sometimes I feel sure I can reach them, and sometimes I feel uncertain. What should I do?

My dear child, I have placed the desire in you to achieve great goals. I have placed the ability in you to succeed and experience an abundant life. I have created you for a purpose. I will help you fulfill that purpose. Do not let the tentacles of doubt attach themselves to your mind. Read and meditate on My words often. Begin to believe them. Begin to believe in yourself. Begin to believe Me. Then you will gain strength and power to overcome your lack of confidence, and experience good success.

The thief's purpose is to steal and kill and destroy. My purpose is to give them a rich and satisfying life. (John 10:10)

"For I know the plans I have for you," says the LORD. "They are plans for good and not for disaster, to give you a future and a hope." (Jeremiah 29:11)

You are my hope, O Almighty Lord. You have been my confidence ever since I was young. (Psalm 71:5 GW)

For the Lord shall be thy confidence. (Proverbs 3:26 KJV)

You Can Choose to Say No to

Anxiety

Dear Heavenly Father, there are times when I become anxious about the present, my future, my school exams or schedule, or family situations. I sometimes have trouble sleeping, or become jittery and nervous. I don't like feeling this way. Can You help me?

My precious child, your feelings and emotions are real. I created them. However, I created you to live life free from concern, stress, or worry. When you begin to feel these emotions, remain calm, take a deep breath. I have many words to help you overcome. Call My name often. I will help you remain calm in the midst of your anxiety.

Do not be anxious about your life.
(Matthew 6:25 ESV)

When anxiety was great within me,
Your consolation brought me joy. (Psalm 94:19 NIV)

Say to those with anxious heart,
"Take courage, and fear not." (Isaiah 35:4)

Therefore do not be anxious about tomorrow.
(Matthew 6:34 ESV)

Do not be anxious about anything.
(Philippians 4:6 NIV)

You Can Choose to Say No to
Impurity

The Centers for Disease Control and Prevention reports that *"nearly 20 million new sexually transmitted infections occur every year in this country ... Each of these infections is a potential threat to an individual's immediate and long-term health and well-being."*[1]

Heavenly Father, there is the temptation everywhere to not remain pure. Movies, ads, and friends all broadcast tempting images. I want to commit to purity. Give me the strength to overcome the sins that seem so enjoyable.

My child, I created you with emotions, not for them to control you, but for you to control them. If you say no to impurity, you'll preserve your precious and wonderfully made body, physically and spiritually. Wait for that special one you'll spend the rest of your life with in the sacred union of marriage. Treat your body like a cared for, precious, irreplaceable, and unique diamond. Read my Word; develop a daily relationship with Me. You will find strength to overcome momentary enjoyment in exchange for your "long-term health and well-being."

Run from sexual sin! No other sin so clearly affects the body as this one does. For sexual immorality is a sin against your own body. (I Corinthians 6:18)

He who commits adultery lacks sense; he who does it destroys himself. (Proverbs 6:32 ESV)

Create in me a pure heart, O God. (Psalm 51:10 NIV)

Turn my eyes from worthless things. (Psalm 139:37)

[1]http://www.cnn.com/2014/01/09/us/west-virginia-contaminated-water/

You Can Choose to Say No to
Bad Manners

Listed here are ten important points regarding good manners based on *Etiquette for Dummies by Sue Fox:*

1. Be respectful to others including elders, family members, people of other religions and cultures, and people with disabilities.

2. Make saying, "please," "thank you," "excuse me," and "I am sorry," a habit. Avoid talking back, interrupting, and walking away during a conversation.

3. Treat people the way you would like to be treated.

4. Maintain daily cleanliness: shower or bathe, brush teeth, comb hair, exercise, get enough sleep, and wear appropriate clean and neat clothing.

5. Help with household chores: taking out trash, setting the table, help with pets, and keeping room tidy.

6. When meeting others, introduce yourself by saying your name in a clear voice. Relax, and speak in a normal voice. You may also extend your right hand in a greeting handshake while introducing yourself. Hold the person's entire hand, fingers, and palm where the thumbs meet and cross each other. Then squeeze firmly and shake three times, being sure to look into the other person's eyes.

7. Practice table manners: wait until all are seated at the table before beginning to eat, don't grab food, wait for dishes to be passed around the table, and talk about pleasant subjects.

8. When invited to a friend's house, be a gracious guest. You may also write a thank-you note after the visit. Be a gracious host. Greet your guests, take coats, and welcome them to your home.

9. Respect all cultures. We live in a multicultural world made up of different race and religions.

10. Focus on the positive. Manners and etiquette are important because they are really acts of kindness and consideration for others.

Do to others as you would like them to do to you.
(Luke 6:31)

You Can Choose to Say No to
Not Feeling Loved

Heavenly Father, there are times when I feel misunderstood, unaccepted, rejected, insecure, and unloved.

Dear Child, to overcome those feelings, be assured, I understand you. I accept you. I will never reject you. Let your security be in Me. I love you. Begin to remind yourself each day of how I see you. Set aside a few moments to read my words. Listen as I speak to your heart:

I know you by your name.[1] I formed you before you were in your mother's womb.[2] My thoughts of you are more than the sand on the seashore.[3] I know how many strands of hair are on your head.[4] You are the apple of My eye.[5] You are My masterpiece.[6] You are of value to Me.[7] I accept you.[8] You are precious in My sight.[9] My cross is the proof of the intense love I have for you.[10] Nothing can separate you from that love.[11] It has no end, and will last forever.[12]

[1]Isaiah 43:1; [2]Jeremiah 1:5; [3]Psalm 139:17-18
[4]Luke 12:7; [5]Zechariah 2:8; [6]Ephesians 2:10
[7]Matthew 10:31; [8]Ephesians 1:6; [9]Isaiah 43:4
[10]1John 3:16; [11]Romans 8:38-39; [12]Jeremiah 31:3

The Greatest
Relationship

The greatest relationship you will ever have is a personal relationship with Jesus Christ. Healing, forgiveness, deliverance, peace, and restoration can be yours.

The One who calls you special, precious, treasured, and beloved, loves you beyond measure, and wants to walk with you and talk with you every day of your life.

Here is a prayer that can change your life. Pray it—or something like it—from the bottom of your heart today and begin your relationship with Jesus Christ:

Father, You have promised that if I confess my sin, You will forgive me and cleanse me from all the wrong things I've done (1 John 1:9). I confess now. Forgive me. Fill me with Your Holy Spirit. Take my hand and walk with me for the rest of my life. In Jesus' name, amen.

About the Author

As an author and speaker, Merle M. Mills, founder of *Changed through the Word*, ministers throughout Hampton Roads sharing the good news of a changed life through words from the Holy Scriptures. Her prayer is that her reading and listening audience will allow the power of God the freedom to do the same in and through their lives. Her other books can be found on amazon.com.

Merle lives with her family in Norfolk, Virginia.

Changed Through the Word
P. O. Box 41293
Norfolk, VA 23541

www.changedthrutheword.org
www.changedthrutheword.blogspot.com
www.nomoreasecret.blogspot.com
email: changedthrutheword@gmail.com
You can also find Changed Thru The Word on Facebook.

Made in the USA
San Bernardino, CA
24 June 2016